EQUIPPING THE CHURCH FOR THE HARVEST

Practical Evangelism Teaching To Empower The Church

Dr. Aaron Jones

EQUIPPING THE CHURCH FOR THE HARVEST

All rights reserved. No part of this book may be reproduced or transmitted in any form or by any means, electronic or mechanical, including photocopying, recording or by any information storage and retrieval system without written permission from the author, except for the inclusion of brief quotations in a review.

All scripture quotations are from the King James Version of the Bible. Thomas Nelson Publishers, Nashville: Thomas Nelson, Inc. 1972.

Copyright © 2009
Dr. Aaron Jones
Printed in the United States of America
ISBN: 978-0-615-33746-3

Editor: Sharon Jones
Drawings: Zara Whitelock

Printed by Morris Publishing
3212 E. Highway 30
Kearney, NE 68847
1-800-650-7888
Equipping the Church for the Harvest

TABLE OF CONTENTS

Part One — Evangelism Foundation   **PAGE**
- Mission — 3
- The Commandment — 4
- The Requirement — 6
- 10 Facts About Evangelism — 8
- The Romans Road to Salvation — 9
- The Reality of an Unbeliever — 11
- Questions — 12

Part Two — God's Perspective on Evangelism and Souls
- The Heart of God in Evangelism — 15
- The Power of God in Evangelism — 16
- The Increase of God in Evangelism — 17
- Evangelism Has No Boundaries (What, When, Where, How) — 18
- Eight Keys to Evangelism — 19
- Questions — 21

Part Three — Methods of Evangelism
- Evangelism Outside the Church — 24
- Two-By-Two Rule — 25
- Do's and Don'ts to When Dealing with an Unbeliever — 26
- Excuses of An Unbeliever — 27
- Excuses of a Non-Believer — 28

Part Four — One-on-One Evangelism
- Practical Evangelism — 29
- The Sinner's Prayer — 32

Part Five — Statistical Reports
- Evangelism Questionnaire — 33
- Evangelism Demographics — 34
- Evangelism Status Form — 36
- Evangelism Follow-Up Profile — 37
- Evangelism Survey — 38
- After Evangelism Review (AER) — 39
- Sample Tracts — 40

Part Six — Questions and Answers — 43

PART ONE
Evangelism Foundation

THE MISSION

The Great Commission found in Matthew 28:18-20 has become the mission of the Church. The mission of the church is to carry out the commandment of Jesus Christ found in Holy Scriptures (Acts 1:8, Mark 16:15, Matthew 28:18-20).

The success of the church cannot only be measured in the size of a church, the amount of activities of a church, or even, in the number of members in a church. The success of the church should be measured on how well it obeys the Great Commission.

God has not only called the church to evangelize the world, but He has called each individual believer to witness the good news of the gospel. God doesn't want evangelism to be just another event, but a way of life. We must understand that not all are called to be an Evangelist (Ephesians 4:11), but all are called to evangelize (Acts 1:8).

The mission of the church is to seek the unsaved and the unchurched in the community; and to exercise all diligence in leading them into a saving knowledge of Jesus Christ and the fellowship of the church; and to make known God's love to all mankind.

THE COMMANDMENT

Jesus' last words to His disciples...

Matthew 28:18-20

18 "And Jesus came and spake unto them, Saying, all power is given unto me in heaven and in earth. 19 Go ye therefore, and teach all nations, baptizing them in the name of the Father, and of the Son, and of the Holy Ghost: 20 Teaching them to observe all things whatsoever I have commanded you: and lo, I am with you always, even unto the end of the world."

Just as Jesus commanded His disciples to go, spread the gospel, and make more disciples; this commandment is extended to the church. The church is to spread the good news of Jesus; and to guide the new converts into being disciples for the kingdom.

Jesus' last words were not a request, but a command. Remember as we obey Him, Jesus is with us always through His Holy Spirit.

Mark 16:15

"And he said unto them, Go ye into all the world, and preach the gospel to every creature."

Jesus did not say select who you wish (particularly those you think would be receptive), but preach to all people that Christ paid the price for their sins; and that those who believe in Him can be forgiven and live eternally with God.

THE REQUIREMENT

There are three major requirements to salvation: (1) Decision; (2) Confession; and (3) Belief.

Let's analyze Romans 10:9 which says, *"That if thou shalt confess with the mouth Lord Jesus, and shalt believe in thine heart that God hath raised him from the dead, thou shalt be saved."*

A DECISION

We must make a decision to choose God or Satan, to choose eternal life or eternal damnation. Our decision must be clear and concise. Reason being, we cannot choose both God and Satan. God wants us to freely choose him above all other choices.

A CONFESSION

There must be an open confession with our mouth that Jesus is Lord. When we confess Jesus is Lord, we are ready to allow Jesus to be ruler, master, and owner of our lives. This confession should lead to true repentance (a turning away from our old ways and walking in God ways).

A BELIEF

We must believe (from the heart) in the redemptive work of Jesus:

1. God sent His only begotten Son from glory (John 17:5, John 3:16).

2. Jesus walked on this earth (John 1:14).

3. Jesus hung on the cross for the sins of world (John 19:18).

4. Jesus died on the cross and rose again on the third day (John 19:31-33).

5. Jesus is coming back for all those who are saved (I Thessalonians 4:13-18).

10 FACTS ABOUT EVANGELISM

1. Evangelism has no boundaries.

2. Evangelism has no respect of person.

3. Evangelism involves the teaching of the Gospel.

4. Evangelism must be led by the Holy Spirit.

5. Evangelism must be done in your community.

6. Evangelism brings repentance.

7. Evangelism involves preaching and teaching.

8. Evangelism is limited to one message, but has different methods.

9. Evangelism involves being active.

10. Evangelism involves a promise from Jesus Christ, "*I am always with* you…"

THE ROMANS ROAD TO SALVATION

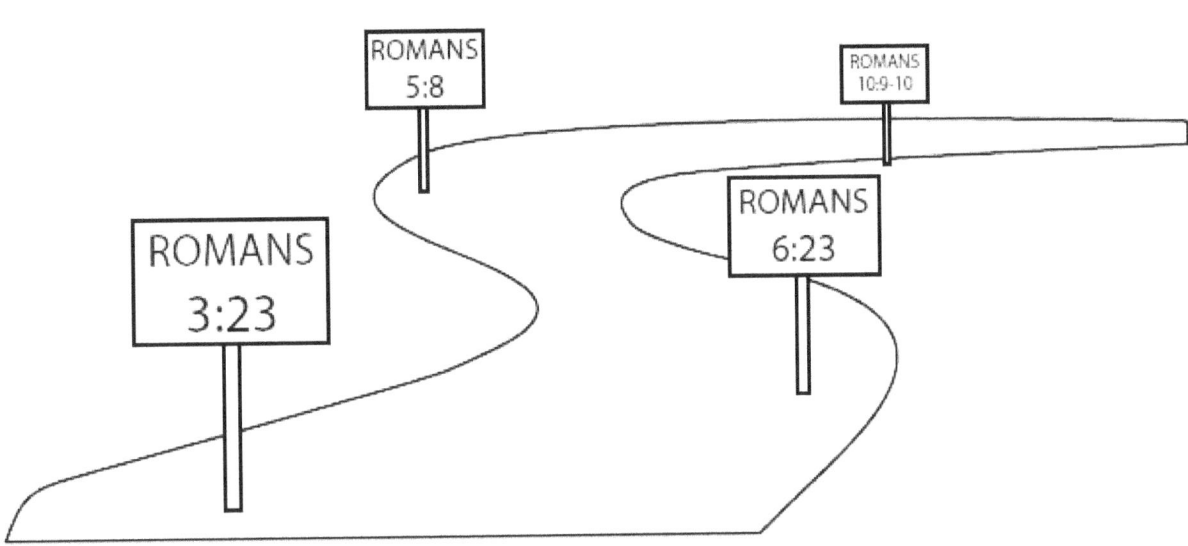

Because of the fall of man in the Garden of Eden, mankind will go through the process of the "Romans Road" to salvation. The Book of Romans identifies the reality of man's position without God, a sinner in need of a savior. It explains the love and grace of God for the life of every person. God extends His love to all people. If man decides not to chose God or His love, death is the alternative.

ROAD #1– ALL ARE SINNERS AND IN NEED OF A SAVIOR.

Romans 3:23 —*"For all have sinned, and come short of the glory of God."*

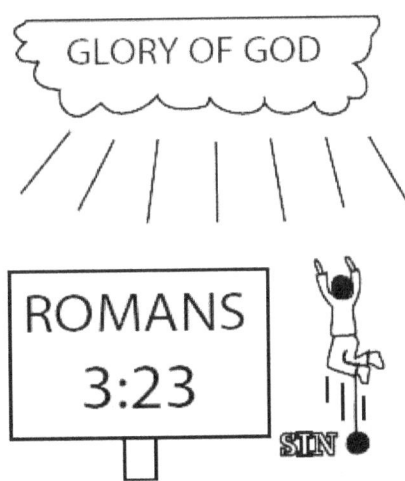

ROAD #2 – THE PENALTY OF SIN IS DEATH.

Romans 6:23 —*"For the wages of sin is death; but the gift of God is eternal life through Jesus Christ our Lord."*

ROAD #3 – JESUS' EXPRESSION OF LOVE WAS TO DIE FOR OUR SINS.

Romans 5:8 —*"But God commendeth his love toward us, in that, while we were yet sinners, Christ died for us."*

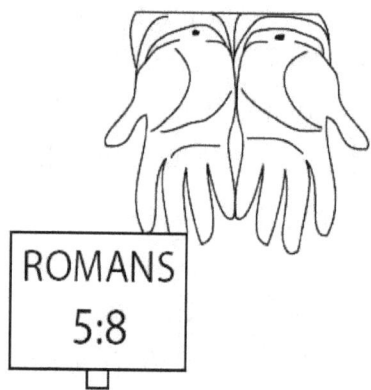

ROAD #4 – SALVATION COMES THROUGH A CONFESSION AND A BELIEF OF JESUS' WORK ON THE CROSS.

Romans 10:9, 10 —*"That if thou shalt confess with thy mouth the Lord Jesus, that God hath raised him from the dead, thou shalt be saved. For with the heart man believeth unto righteousness; and with the mouth confession is made unto salvation."*

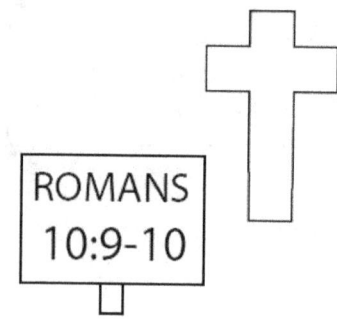

THE REALITY OF AN UNBELIEVER

1. **THE UNBELIEVER MUST REALIZE HE OR SHE IS LOST.**
   II Corinthians 4:4 —*"In whom the god of this world hath blinded the minds of them which believe not, lest the light of the glorious gospel of Christ, who is the image of God, should shine unto them."*

   Until an unbeliever enters into a relationship with Jesus Christ he is blinded by the enemy. An unbeliever sinner must know he needs to be found. When an unbeliever realizes he is lost his sins, it is then that he accepts the free gift of eternal life.

2. **THE UNBELIEVER MUST WANT TO BE SAVED.**
   Acts 16:27-30 —*"And the **keeper of the prison** awaking out of his sleep, and seeing the prison doors open, he drew out his sword, and would have killed himself, supposing that the prisoners had been fled. But Paul cried with a loud voice, saying, Do thyself no harm: for we are all here. Then he called for a light, and sprang in, and came trembling, and fell down before Paul and Silas. And brought them out, and said, Sirs, **what must I do to be saved**?*

   Once an unbeliever sinner realizes he is lost, he must want to be found. Not until a person opens his heart to God can salvation take place. They must want to replace the life that is leading to eternal separation from God, to a life that pleases God.

3. **THE UNBELIEVER MUST REPENT OF HIS AND BELIEVE IN JESUS CHRIST FOR SALVATION.**
   Matthew 3:1, 2 —*"In those days came John the Baptist, preaching in the wilderness of Judea, and saying, Repent ye: for the kingdom of heaven is at hand."*

   Once an unbeliever realizes he is lost and wants to be saved, then repentance must take place. No matter what time of year or day, God's kingdom is always at hand. The unbeliever must seize the moment: *"Seek ye the Lord while he may be found, call ye upon him while he is near"* (Isaiah 55:6).

PART ONE QUESTIONS

THE MISSION (TRUE OR FALSE)

1. _____ Evangelism should be a way of life.

2. _____ All believers are called to evangelize.

3. _____ The success of the church should always be measured by church growth.

4. _____ The mission of the church is the Great Commission.

5. _____ All believers are called to be an Evangelist.

THE COMMANDMENT

1. Who has been given all power (Matthew 28:18)?

   _____

2. Who are the believers teaching (Matthew 28:19)?

   _____

3. What are believers teaching (Matthew 28:20)?

   _____

4. What is the promise of evangelism (Matthew 28:20)?

   _____

THE REQUIREMENT (FILL IN THE BLANK)

1. The non-believer must choose between _____ and _____ in order to see God.

2. What are the two outcomes of choosing God or Satan?

   _____ _____ or _____ _____

3. God sent His only begotten _____ from glory (John 17:5, John 3:16).

4. Jesus walked on this _____ (John 1:14).

5. Jesus hung on the cross for the _____ of the world (John 19:18).

6. Jesus died on the cross and rose again on the _____ _____ (John 19:31-33).

7. Jesus is _____ back for all those who are saved (I Thessalonians 4:13-18).

8. A true confession leads to a true _____.

9. The non-believer must confess with his _____ and believe in his _____ that Jesus is Lord.

FACTS ABOUT EVANGELISM (TRUE OR FALSE)

1. _____ Evangelism should only take place in the church.

2. _____ There is only one method to evangelism.

3. _____ The foundation of evangelism is the Gospel.

4. _____ Evangelism is only for good people.

THE ROMANS ROAD (FILL IN THE BLANK)

1. _____ has sinned before God (Romans 3:23).

2. The wages of sin is _____ (Romans 6:23).

3. The gift of God is eternal _____ (Romans 6:23).

4. While we were sinners Christ _____ for us (Romans 5:8).

5. Salvation requires a confession with the _____ (Romans 10:9).

THE REALITY OF THE UNBELIEVER

1. Who has blinded the unbeliever (II Corinthians 4:4)?

   _____ _____ _____ _____ _____

2. The _____ _____ must shine to bring sinners to the saving knowledge of the truth (II Corinthians 4:4).

3. A unbeliever must realize he is _____ before coming to salvation.

4. "_____ for the kingdom of heaven is at hand (Matthew 3:2)."

5. The keeper of the prison said, "what must I do to be _____ (Acts 16:30)."

PART TWO
God's Perspective on Evangelism and Souls

THE HEART OF GOD IN EVANGELISM

THE HEART OF GOD

II Peter 3:9 —*"The Lord is not slack concerning his promise, as some men count slackness; but is longsuffering to usward, not willing that any should perish, but that all should come to repentance."*

_____

_____

_____

II Timothy 2:4 —*"Who will have all men to be saved, and to come unto the knowledge of the truth."*

_____

_____

_____

THE POWER OF GOD IN EVANGELISM

THE POWER OF GOD

Acts 1:8 —*"But ye shall receive power, after that the Holy Ghost is come upon you: and ye shall be witnesses unto me both in Jerusalem, and in all Judea, and in Samaria, and unto the uttermost part of the earth."*

_____

_____

_____

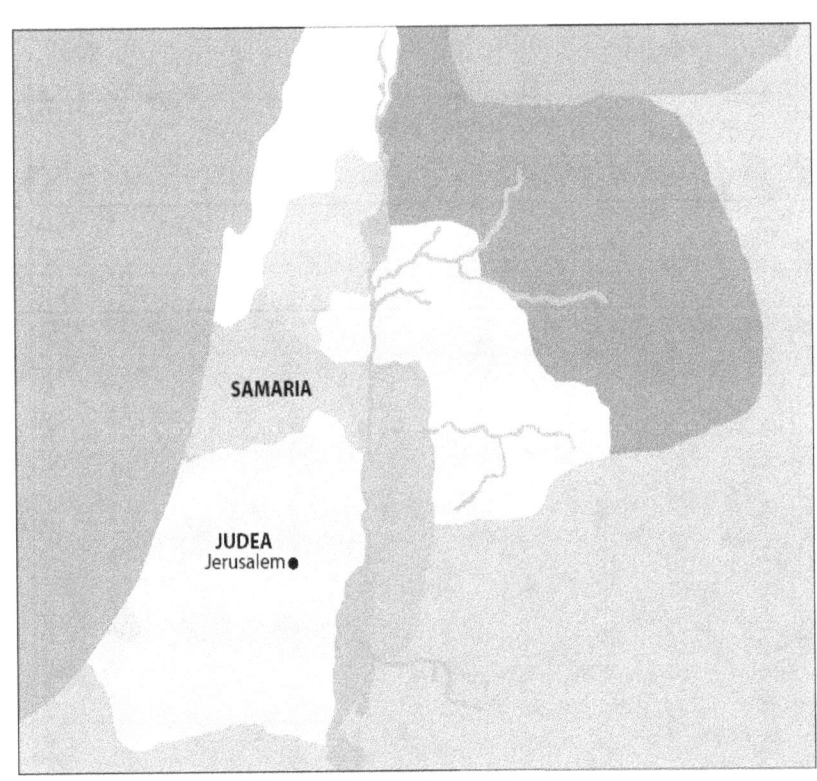

THE INCREASE OF GOD IN EVANGELISM

THE INCREASE OF GOD

II Corinthians 3:6 —*"I have planted, Apollos watered; but God gave the increase."*

_____

_____

_____

EVANGELISM HAS NO BOUNDARIES

(Where, When, What, and How)

- **TO ALL NATIONS** (Where and What)
  Matthew 28:19 —*"Go ye therefore, and teach all nations, baptizing in the name of the Father, and of the Son, and of the Holy Ghost."*

  _____
  _____
  _____

- **HOUSE TO HOUSE** (Where and What)
  Acts 5:42—*"And daily in the temple, and in every house, they ceased not to teach and preach Jesus Christ."*

  _____
  _____
  _____

- **ALWAYS** (When)
  I Peter 3:15—*"But sanctify the Lord God in your hearts: and be ready always to give an answer to every man that asketh you a reason of the hope that is in you with meekness and fear."*

  _____
  _____
  _____

- **AS AMBASSADORS** (How)
  II Corinthians 5:20—*"Now then we are ambassadors for Christ, as though God did beseech you by us: we pray you in Christ's stead, be ye reconciled to God."*

  _____
  _____
  _____

EIGHT KEYS TO EVANGELISM

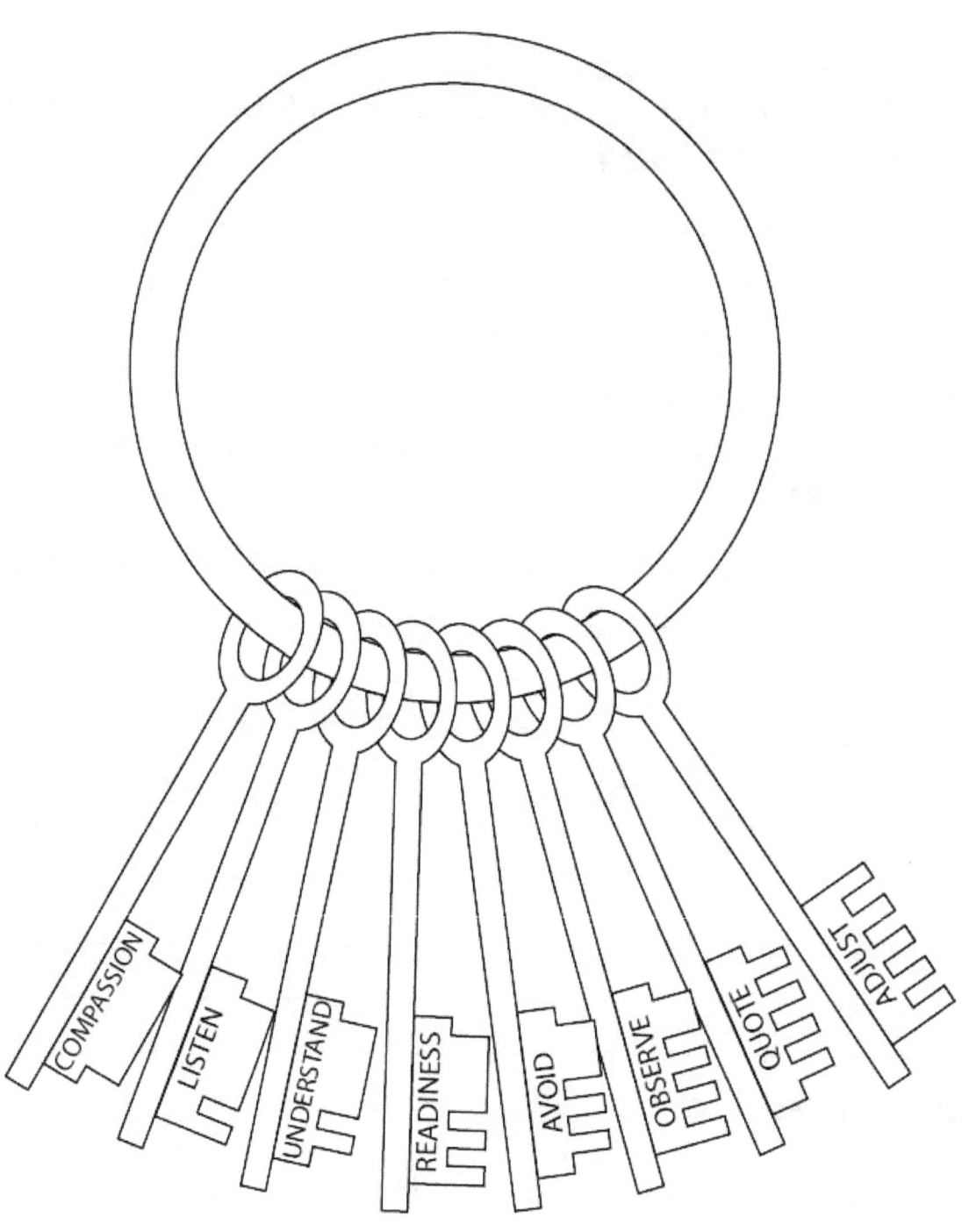

EIGHT KEYS TO EVANGELISM

KEY #1 — Express Compassion.
Jude 22 says, *"And of some have compassion making a difference."*

KEY #2 — Know How To Listen.
James 1:19 says, *"Wherefore, my beloved brethren, let every man be swift to hear, slow to speak, slow to wrath."*

KEY #3 — Understand the Mindset of the Unbeliever.
Romans 12:2 says, *"And be not conformed to this world: but be ye transformed by the renewing of your mind."*

KEY #4 — Be Ready.
I Peter 3:15 says, *"But sanctify the Lord God in your hearts: and be ready always to give an answer to every man that asketh you a reason of the hope that is in you with meekness and fear."*

KEY #5 — Avoid Confrontational Conversation.
Titus 3:9 *says, "But avoid foolish questions, and genealogies, and contentions, and strivings about he law; for they are unprofitable and vain."*

KEY #6 — Observe Body Gestures and Countenances.
Genesis 4:6 *says, "And the Lord said unto Cain, Why art thou wroth? And why is thy countenance fallen?"*

KEY #7 — Never Say "The Bible Says" Unless You Know and Can Quote the Scripture.
II Timothy 2:15 *says, "Study to show thyself approved unto God, a workman that needeth not to be ashamed, rightly dividing the word of truth."*

KEY #8 — Adjust For Individuality.
Genesis 1:26 *says, "And God said, Let us make man in our image, after our likeness."*

PART TWO QUESTIONS

THE HEART OF GOD

1. Whose promises are being referenced in II Peter 3:9?
   _____

2. Who is God displaying longsuffering to (II Peter 3:9)?
   _____

3. Who is able to come to repentance (I Timothy 2:4)?
   _____

4. Explain the Heart of God.
   _____
   _____
   _____
   _____

THE POWER OF GOD

1. Who is the source of your power when it comes to evangelism (Acts 1:8)?
   _____

2. Who should be witnesses of the Gospel (Acts 1:8)?
   _____

3. Who should be witnesses of the Gospel (Acts 1:8)?
   _____

THE INCREASE OF GOD

1. Who is doing the planting of the gospel (II Corinthians 3:6)?
   _____

2. Who is doing the watering of the gospel (II Corinthians 3:6)?
   _____

3. Who is responsible for the increase (II Corinthians 3:6)?
   _____

4. What is the message of II Corinthians 3:6 as it pertains to evangelism?
   _____
   _____
   _____

8 KEYS TO EVANGELISM

Place the appropriate by each key.

1. _____   Express Compassion
2. _____   Know How to Listen
3. _____   Understand the Unbeliever's Mindset
4. _____   Be Ready
5. _____   Avoid Confrontational Conversation
6. _____   Observe Body Gestures and Countenances
7. _____   Quote
8. _____   Individuality

A. James 1:19 — *"Wherefore, my beloved brethren, let every man be swift to hear, slow to speak, slow to wrath" Before we get angry or even speak, we are to listen."*

B. Jude 22 — *"And of some have compassion making a difference."*

C. Titus 3:9 — *"But avoid foolish questions, and genealogies, and contentions, and strivings about he law; for they are unprofitable and vain."*

D. Timothy 2: 15 — *"Study to show thyself approved unto God, a workman that needeth not to be ashamed, rightly dividing the word of Truth."*

E. Romans 12:2 — *"And be not conformed to this world: but be ye transformed by the renewing of your mind."*

F. Genesis 1:26 — *"And God said, Let us make man in our image, after our likeness."*

G. Genesis 4:6 — *"And the Lord said unto Cain, Why art thou wroth? And why is thy countenance fallen?"*

H. I Peter 3:15 — *"But sanctify the Lord God in your hearts: and be ready always to give an answer to every man that asketh you a reason of the hope that is in you with meekness and fear."*

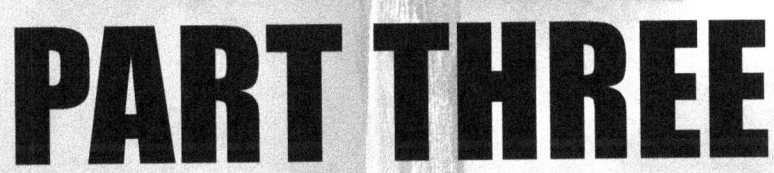

PART THREE
Methods of Evangelism

EVANGELISM OUTSIDE THE CHURCH

The call of evangelism is not only a call to the church, but a call to every born again believer. The church must be the extension of God's love to a dying world. We must go to places that are uncomfortable; we must speak to individuals we don't know; we must encourage people even we don't condone their past, we must place needs of others before our own; and we must visit people that society has forgotten. In Matthew 25:35, 36, Jesus says, *"For I was hungred, and ye gave me meat: I was thirsty, and ye gave me drink: I was a stranger, and ye took me in. Naked, and ye clothed me: I was sick, and ye visited me: I was in prison, and ye came unto me."* God wants the church to take the Good News of Jesus Christ outside the four walls of the church. There is a tremendous harvest outside the doors of the church.

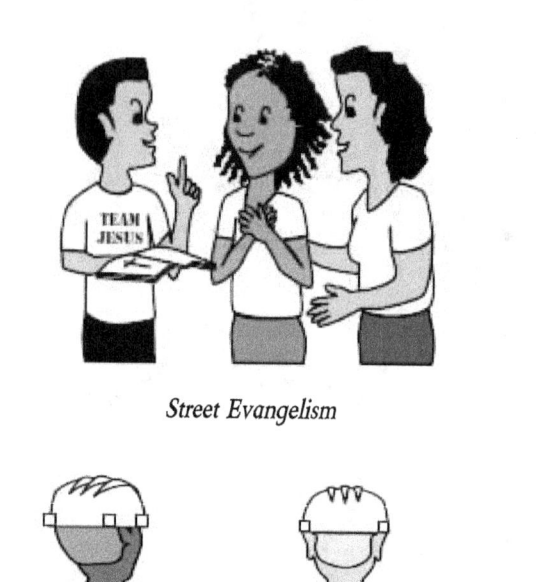
Street Evangelism

Prison Evangelism

Job Evangelism

Nursing/Hospital Evangelism

It is important to remember consistency, listening ear, encouraging words, common ground, one-on-one spiritual guidance, prayer, being a living example, and teaching/preaching the gospel are vital to ministry outside the church walls.

TWO-BY-TWO RULE

"And he called unto him the twelve, and began to send them forth by two and two; and gave them power over unclean spirits" (Mark 6:7).

WHY THE TWO-BY-TWO RULE:

- Jesus sent the His disciples out in 2's — Jesus strategically sent out the disciples in twos. He understands the need for one to strengthen and encourage the other while on a mission.

- To have a witness — witnesses confirm the work of the Holy Spirit and any other activities while evangelizing.

- One person is always praying — it leaves one person available to intercede; praying for the Holy Spirit to intervene.

- Protection — it is important to have extra eyes to be mindful of any surrounding activity.

- Connection — it provides greater opportunity for a connection to be made with a variety of people that are encountered.

DO'S AND DON'TS WHEN DEALING WITH AN UNBELIEVER

- Don't approach an unbeliever in a superior attitude.

- Do approach an unbeliever in the Spirit of God's love and grace.

- Don't approach an unbeliever with intentions to be judgmental.

- Do approach an unbeliever in the Spirit of joy.

- Don't make light with an unbeliever about becoming a Christian.

- Do live before them as an example of Jesus Christ.

- Don't approach an unbeliever in a confrontational spirit.

- Do intercede daily for the unbeliever.

- Do find other people close to the unbeliever.

- Do stay in contact as much as possible with the unbeliever.

EXCUSES OF AN UNBELIEVER

- "I am not ready to commit my life to a church." What is your response?

　

　

　

- "What if I backslide?" What is your response?

　

　

　

- "The church is filled with men and women living two different lives." What is your response?

　

　

　

- "I will never be good enough to be called a Christian. A Christian should be perfect." What is your response?

EXCUSES OF A NON-BELIEVER

- "I must give up all fun in my life to become a Christian." What is your response?

  _____
  _____
  _____

- "I have time to make a decision about Jesus in my life." What is your response?

  _____
  _____
  _____

- "The Bible cannot be true." What is your response?

  _____
  _____
  _____

PART FOUR
One-on-One Evangelism

PRACTICAL EVANGELISM

PE #1: You approach a stranger and say "Good morning!" His response, "What is so good about it?"

How would you respond?

_____
_____
_____
_____
_____
_____

PE #2: A family member or friend approaches you and says, "What difference will it make if I accept Jesus, my life is not going to change."

How would you respond?

_____
_____
_____
_____
_____
_____

PE #3: Express Compassion

Linda attends her family reunion every year. Every year, faithfully, she witnesses to her family; but she receives negative responses. She has decided that it is useless to witness to her family and has decided not to witness anymore. She states, "I will leave them to their own sinful way."

What should Linda have done differently?

_____
_____
_____
_____
_____
_____

PE #4: Know How to Listen

Mark has worked at government agencies for ten years. Mark is a good Christian man. On his breaks, Mark makes it a priority to witness to everyone he comes in contact with, on his job. When Mark was entering into the lounge, he noticed Mary, his co-worker, eating. Mary does not attend church because of personal reasons. When Mark begins to witness to her, Mary responds, "All church people are hypocrites." Mark did not allow Mary to finish her statement.

Should Mark have responded differently? Explain.

_____
_____
_____
_____
_____
_____

PE #5: Understanding the Unbeliever's Mindset

Kathy's parents took her to church faithfully every Sunday. When Kathy was 16 years-old, her parents were killed in a car accident. She has not been to church since. Kathy is now 29-years old and still misses her mother and father. She believed for years, "If there was a God, why would He allow both of my parents to die?" Michael is out evangelizing with his church and meets Kathy. He gives her a tract and Kathy responds, "There is no such thing as God." Michael thinks, "How can anyone make such a statement?" and walks saying, "I will pray for you."

How should have Michael responded?

_____

_____

_____

_____

_____

_____

A SINNER'S PRAYER

Lord, I am sorry and I repent of all my sins, known and unknown. Lord, please forgive me of all my sins; and wash me whiter than snow. I confess that you can be Lord and Savior of my life. I believe in my heart that you did die on the cross for my sins. I believe in my heart that you rose from the dead on the third day. I believe you are coming back for me. Thank you Lord for give me another chance. In Jesus Name, Amen.

"I am an ALCOHOLIC"   "I am a PROSTITUTE"   "I am a DRUG ADDICT"

PART FIVE
Statistical Reports

EVANGELISM QUESTIONAIRE

1. How many people do you encounter on an average day?
   _____

2. Of those same people, how many do you see and communicate with everyday?
   _____

3. Of those same people, how many are family members?
   _____

5. Of those same people, how many are friends?
   _____

7. Of those same people, how many are co-workers?
   _____

8. Of those same people, how many are strangers?
   _____

9. Of those same people, how many are unsaved?
   _____

EVANGELISM DEMOGRAPHICS

1. Location of Community

   _____

   _____

2. Number of churches in the community   _____

3. Number of people in the community   _____

4. Average age of the community:
   - ☐ 0-5
   - ☐ 6-12
   - ☐ 13-18
   - ☐ 19-25
   - ☐ 26-35
   - ☐ 36-45
   - ☐ 46-55
   - ☐ 56 and older

5. Marital Status of the community:
   - ☐ Married
   - ☐ Single
   - ☐ Divorced
   - ☐ Other

6. Economic Status of the community:
   - ☐ Low Income
   - ☐ Middle Class
   - ☐ Upper Class

7. Educational Status of the Community:
   - ☐ No High School Diploma
   - ☐ High School Diploma/GED
   - ☐ Some College
   - ☐ Undergraduate Degree
   - ☐ Graduate Degree

8. Religious Background/Preferences of the Community:
   - ☐ Unchurched
   - ☐ Churched
   - ☐ Denominations

   _____

   _____

   _____

   _____

9. External Factors:
   - ☐ Liquor Stores
   - ☐ Gangs
   - ☐ Lack of Recreational Facilities
   - ☐ Others

   _____

   _____

   _____

   _____

EVANGELISM STATUS FORM

Date: _____

Type of Evangelism: ☐ Street   ☐ Hospital/Nursing   ☐ Home
                     ☐ Door to Door   ☐ Service   ☐ Prison
                     ☐ Other _____

NAME	PRAYER	FELLOWSHIP	CONVERSATION	OTHER

List Name/Action Taken: _____

_____

Follow-Up Date: _____   Follow-Up Event: _____

EVANGELISM FOLLOW UP PROFILE

Name: _____

Address: _____

City: _____ State: _____ Zip Code: _____

Home Phone #: _____ Cell Phone #: _____

Action Taken:

_____
_____
_____
_____

Converted: ☐ Yes or ☐ No

Notes (Brief History/Circumstances):

_____
_____
_____
_____
_____
_____

EVANGELISM SURVEY

1. Of what religious group or church are you a member?
   - ☐ Baptist
   - ☐ Catholic
   - ☐ Christian Church
   - ☐ Christian Science
   - ☐ Lutheran
   - ☐ Episcopal
   - ☐ Jewish
   - ☐ Mormon
   - ☐ Methodist
   - ☐ Presbyterian
   - ☐ Other

2. What local church do you attend? _____

3. How often do you attend?
   - ☐ Weekly
   - ☐ Sometimes
   - ☐ Seldom
   - ☐ Never

4. Do you believe you are going to Heaven, Hell, or neither?

   _____
   _____
   _____
   _____

5. Why?

   _____
   _____
   _____
   _____

AFTER EVANGELISM REVIEW (AER)

1. What was the mission?

   _____

   _____

   _____

2. Was the mission accomplished?

   _____

   _____

   _____

3. What did we do right while on the mission?

   _____

   _____

   _____

4. What did we do wrong while on the mission?

   _____

   _____

   _____

5. What do we need to improve regarding mission?

   _____

   _____

   _____

SAMPLE TRACTS

Sample #1: Free Medicine

_____ CHURCH NAME _____ ADDRESS _____ PHONE #	God sent His Only Begotten Son to provide an answer to the sin in your life.	No matter what you are struggling with, God is willing to work with you. Confess Jesus tody and receive your... **FREE MEDICINE!**	**FREE MEDICINE!** 
If  is a sickness Then WE are all SICK!	Romans 3:23 says, "For all have sinned, and fallen short of the glory of God."  GOD'S GLORY	Everyone that walks on this earth has and will sin, but there is good news. We do not have to live in this fallen state. The cure for sickness is free of charge.	Romans 3:24 says, "Being justified freely by His grace through the redemption that is in Christ Jesus." Jesus + 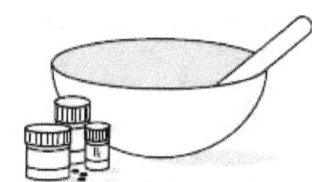 = Redemptive Grace

SAMPLE TRACTS

Sample #2: Heart Transplant

Psalm 51:10 says, *"Create in me a clean heart, O God; and renew a right spirit within me."* Open your heart today and receive His Son as your personal Savior. It is time for a heart transplant!

CHURCH NAME

ADDRESS

PHONE #

ARE YOU HAVING HEART PROBLEMS?

Does your heart posses love and forgiveness? Does your love extend to an Almighty God and your forgiveness to an imperfect man?

God wants to give the world a heart transplant.

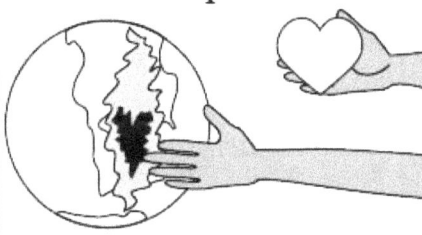

He wants everyone to have His heart. God's heart is based solely on an unconditional love for mankind. David made it very clear when he saw that he needed open-heart surgery by an Almighty God.

SAMPLE TRACTS

Sample #3: Forgive and Forget

God is willing to forgive you of your sins!

CHURCH NAME

ADDRESS

PHONE #

When was the last time you have hurt someone, and that same person not only forgave you, but they forgot the whole ordeal? When was the last time you wronged someone? Time and time again, do you think that same person will continue to forgive you?

1 John 1:9 says, *"If we confess our sins, He is faithful and just to forgive us our sins, and to cleanse us from all unrighteousness."* God is willing to forget your sins. Isaiah 43:25 says, *"I, even I, am he that blots out thy transgressions for mine own sake, and will not remember thy sins."* Choose Jesus today, and allow God to forgive and forget your sins.

PART SIX

Questions and Answers

PART ONE – ANSWERS

The Mission (True or False)

1. **T** Evangelism should be a way of life.

2. **T** All believers are called to evangelize.

3. **F** The success of the church should always be measured by church growth.

4. **T** The mission of the church is the Great Commission.

5. **F** All believers are called to be an Evangelist.

The Commandment

1. Who has been given all power (Matthew 28:18)?
   Jesus

2. Who are the believers teaching (Matthew 28:19)?
   All Nations

3. What are believers teaching (Matthew 28:20)?
   The Commands of Jesus Christ

4. What is the promise of evangelism (Matthew 28:20)?
   Jesus will be with you always

The Requirement (Fill in the Blank)

1. The non-believer must choose between **God** and **Satan** in order to see God.

2. What are the two outcomes of the choosing God or Satan?
   eternal life or eternal damnation

3. God sent His only begotten **Son** from glory (John 17:5, John 3:16).

4. Jesus walked on this **earth** (John 1:14).

5. Jesus hung on the cross for the **sins** of the world (John 19:18).

6. Jesus died on the cross and rose again on the **third day** (John 19:31-33).

7. Jesus is **coming** back for all those who are saved (I Thessalonians 4:13-18).

8. A true confession leads to a true **confession**.

9. The non-believer must confess with his/her **mouth** and believe in his/her **heart** that Jesus is Lord.

Facts about Evangelism (True or False)

1. **F** Evangelism should only take place in the church.

2. **F** There is only one method to evangelism.

3. **T** The foundation of evangelism is the Gospel.

4. **F** Evangelism is only for good people.

5. **F** Sometimes God is with me when I evangelize.

6. **T** Effective evangelism must involve the Holy Spirit.

The Romans Road (Fill in the Blank)

1. **All** has sinned before God (Romans 3:23).

2. The wages of sin is **death** (Romans 6:23).

3. The gift of God is eternal **life** (Romans 6:23).

4. While we were sinners Christ **died** for us (Romans 5:8).

5. Salvation requires a confession with the **mouth** (Romans 10:9).

The Reality of the Unbeliever

1. Who has blinded the unbeliever (II Corinthians 4:4)?
   The god of this world

2. The **glorious gospel** must shine to bring sinners to the saving knowledge of the truth (II Corinthians 4:4).

3. A unbeliever must realize he/she is **lost** before coming to salvation.

4. "**Repent** for the kingdom of heaven is at hand" (Matthew 3:2).

5. The keeper of the prison said, "what must I do to be **saved** (Acts 16:30)."

PART TWO – ANSWERS

The Heart of God in Evangelism

1. Whose promises are being referenced in II Peter 3:9?
   God's promises

2. Who is God displaying longsuffering to (II Peter 3:9)?
   Usward (mankind)

3. Who is able to come to repentance (I Timothy 2:4)?
   All (the world)

4. Explain Heart of God.
   God does want anyone to perish and spend eternity separated from Him. God wants the world to accept the free gift of His Son, Jesus Christ. His heart for mankind is causing to continuously pour out His grace and mercy over the world.

The Power of God in Evangelism

1. Who is the source of your power when it comes to evangelism (Acts 1:8)?
   Jesus through the Holy Spirit

2. Who should be witnesses of the Gospel (Acts 1:8)?
   All believers

3. Where is your Jerusalem (Acts 1:8)?
   In your community

The Increase of God in Evangelism

1. Who is doing the planting of the gospel (II Corinthians 3:6)?
   All believers

2. Who is doing the watering of the gospel (II Corinthians 3:6)?
   All believers

3. Who is responsible for the increase (II Corinthians 3:6)?
   God

4. What is the message of II Corinthians 3:6 as it pertains to evangelism?
   The Apostle Paul is trying to convey is that the increase of evangelism is God's responsibility. Our responsibility is to plant and water and through Holy Spirit increase will come.

8 Keys to Evangelism
Place the appropriate by each key.

1. **B** Express Compassion
2. **A** Know How to Listen
3. **E** Understand the Unbeliever's Mindset
4. **H** Be Ready
5. **C** Avoid Confrontational Conversation
6. **G** Observe Body Gestures and Countenances
7. **D** Quote
8. **F** Individuality

PART THREE – ANSWERS

- "I am not ready to commit my life to a church."
  A response:
  When you give your life to Jesus this should produce a desire to work in/for the church. Romans 12:1 says, "...present your bodies a living sacrifice, holy, acceptable unto God, which is your reasonable service." When Jesus died on the cross, He gave up His life so that you might have life. You must view this decision not as much as committing your life to the church, but committing your life to Jesus. Was Jesus ready to die? Is anyone ever ready to die to their old ways?

- "What if I backslide?"
  A response:
  If you are trusting God today and is willing to put your life in His hands, backsliding should not be your focus. His grace and mercy has carried this far in your life and His grace is always sufficient; even more so once you accept His free gift of salvation. II Corinthians 12:9 says, "...My grace is sufficient for thee: for my strength is made perfect in weakness..."

- "The church is filled with men and women living two different lives."
  A response:
  What one man or woman does should never be the determining factor whether you come to church or enter into a relationship with Jesus Christ. We all will give an account before God concerning our actions. Romans 14:12 says, "So then every one of us shall give account of himself to God."

- "I will never be good enough to be called a Christian. A Christian should be perfect."
  A response:
  No one by themselves will ever be good enough, but what gives us the right to stand before God is because the work of Jesus Christ on the cross. Romans 3:23 says, "For all have sinned, and come short of the glory of God."

- "I must give up all the fun in my life to become a Christian."
  A response:

  Most of the fun you are speaking of is temporary, it only last for moments. You find greater fun and fulfillment in life when you are living out God's plan for you. This will bring something greater than fun, that is joy and nothing on earth can take that from you. John 14:27 says, Peace I leave with you, my peace I give unto: not as the world giveth, give I unto you..."

- "I have time to make the decision about Jesus in my life."
  A response:

  No one is guaranteed a moment here on earth, this is why we live and make decisions as if it were our last day on earth. There are many decisions we make in life that we think we have more time, but this decision has eternal consequences. We don't know when Jesus will return for us, but we must be ready. Matthew 24:44 say, "Therefore be ye also ready: for in such an hour as ye think not the Son of man cometh."

- "The Bible cannot be all true."
  A response:

  Do you believe any of the Bible to be true? If so, you must believe it is all true. II Timothy 3:16 says, "All scripture is given by inspiration of God..."What part of the Bible you don't believe is true?

PART FOUR – ANSWERS

PE #1: You approach a stranger and say "Good morning!" His response, "What is so good about it?"

How would you respond?

A Suggested Response:
Each day you are able to move and breath is a good day. You have the perfect opportunity, yet a second chance to get right all the wrong from yesterday.

PE #2: A family member or friend approaches you and says, "What difference will it make if I accept Jesus, my life is not going to change."

How would you respond?

A Suggested Response:
Accepting Jesus into your heart will make all the difference. His main purpose for coming to this earth was to bring change into our lives. Have you ever seen a person before they knew Jesus? Once we accept Jesus into our lives, we become new creatures. It is not about what you feel, but what God says. I promise you, if you allow God to change you— He will.

PE #3: Express Compassion

Linda attends her family reunion every year. Every year, faithfully, she witnesses to her family; but she receives negative responses. She has decided that it is useless to witness to her family and has decided not to witness anymore. She states, "I will leave them to their own sinful way."

What should Linda have done differently?

A Suggested Response:

Evangelizing to our family members is and always will be a tough task. Reason being, we have emotional connection with family members. No believer wants to see a family member leave the earth without receiving Jesus as their personal Savior. Tough as it may seem, we do not have the right to leave anyone to themselves. Romans 1:28 says, "And even as they did not like to retain God in their knowledge, God gave them over to a reprobate mind, to do those things which are not convenient." God only has the right to decide when someone is unreachable. We must continue to show love for that family member, and be actively involved in intercession for that person's salvation. There are many ways to intercede for family members without making personal contact with them. Never stop praying for them, petition God daily on their behalf. Whatever you do, try your best not to nag them. Nagging sometimes causes an unbeliever to be resentful to the message and the messenger. Being a godly example is another way to witness to unbelieving family members. Despite their response to you, you must continue to live a Christian life before them. Many Christians hinder their testimony by the way they live before family members. As much as it is within you, live holy before them. Make sure to practice what you preach before them. I Peter 1:15 says, "But as he which hath called you is holy, so be ye holy in all manner of conversation." We are called to be holy in our conversation. Conversation found in this verse means to be holy in our behavior as well. Try not to turn every conversation into a sermon. This may persuade one against the message of Jesus. We must continue to speak in words of love to our unsaved family members; or sometimes their friends can be an avenue of approach. Finally, a card or a letter of love to them, letting them know you still love and care very much about their spiritual well-being.

PE #4: Know How to Listen

Mark has worked at government agencies for ten years. Mark is a good Christian man. On his breaks, Mark makes it a priority to witness to everyone he comes in contact with, on his job. When Mark was entering into the lounge, he noticed Mary, his co-worker, eating. Mary does not attend church because of personal reasons. When Mark begins to witness to her, Mary responds, "All church people are hypocrites." Mark did not allow Mary to finish her statement.

Should Mark have responded differently? Explain.

A Suggested Response:

On the job, it is critical that believers live holy lives. In an environment where majority of the people are unbelievers, they will keep a spotlight on your daily living. One positive not about this scenario is that Mark was witnessing on his time. We must remember to witness to people off the clock as Mark did. Mark's employer is not paying him to witness. Christians should be careful of the time they spend doing God's work on man's time. Please don't misunderstand, Go comes before all things, but there is a time and place for everything. We must be obedient to God's laws and those who have authority over us. Jesus referenced the laws of the land. Matthew 22:21 He said, "Render therefore unto Caesar the things which are Caesar's; and unto God the things that are God's." Although Mark understands that he cannot witness at the expense of his agency, he fails to listen closely to what Mary is really saying. When someone makes a blanket statement, such as "all church people are hypocrites," they may have had a bad experience with the church. When someone has been hurt in a church that may be negative. Marc should have endeavored to find out why Mary feels the way she does. Because Mark did not allow Mary to finish her statement, he didn't find out why she would make such a statement. If Mark had listened to Mary, he might have been able to change her thought about church people. As long as Mary viewed church people as hypocrites, she would not be open to the message of Jesus. Reason being, her primary view of Jesus through the ones she called hypocrites. Listening is more than hearing the words of someone, but it is hearing emotions behind the responses. When Mark stopped Mary from finishing her statement, he did not allow time to thing before speaking. A good listener will study before they speak. Proverbs 18:21 says, "The heart of the righteous studieth to answer...."

PE #5: Understanding the Unbeliever's Mindset

Kathy's parents took her to church faithfully every Sunday. When Kathy was 16-years old, her parents were killed in a car accident. She has not been to church since. Kathy is now 29-years old and still misses her mother and father. She believed for years, "If there was a God, why would He allow both of my parents to die?" Michael is out evangelizing with his church and meets Kathy. He gives her a tract and Kathy responds, "There is no such thing as God." Michael thinks, "How can anyone make such a statement?" and walks saying, "I will pray for you."

How should have Michael responded?

A Suggested Response:

When witnessing we need to be cognizant of an unbeliever. What has taken place in an unbeliever's life should be important to the person who is witnessing. Sometimes we can say the right words at the wrong time and those words will have no affect on the hearer. This can be seen when Michael said he would pray, which was good, but he made this comment as he walked away after making her feel like her thoughts were unimportant. Michael allowed his own mindset and personal opinion to dictate his response. Michael should have inquired as to why Kathy felt that way. I have found, most often in my years of counseling, that a circumstance has come in person's life to cause them to doubt the existence of God. One question Michael could have asked Kathy is "have you always believed there was no God"? If the answer is no, then ask: "At what point did you stop believing?" We want to lead the unbeliever back to the point of belief. As long as Kathy believes God does not exist, anything Michael says will have hard time penetrating her mindset. What controlled Kathy's mindset was the fact that her parents were taken from her and if there was a God, this would not have happened.

NOTES

NOTES

NOTES

NOTES

www.ingramcontent.com/pod-product-compliance
Lightning Source LLC
Chambersburg PA
CBHW081502070526
44586CB00019B/2458